Original title:
Artistic Fusion

Copyright © 2024 Book Fairy Publishing
All rights reserved.

Author: Lisanne Liustik
ISBN HARDBACK: 978-9916-87-171-3
ISBN PAPERBACK: 978-9916-87-172-0
ISBN EBOOK: 978-9916-87-173-7

Threads of Thought

In silken strands we weave our dreams,
A tapestry of hopes and schemes.
Each thread connects with gentle grace,
Creating worlds in this soft space.

Thoughts meander like a stream,
Flowing softly, like a dream.
Intertwined, they spark and glow,
Illuminating all we know.

Whispers dance upon the air,
Telling stories, rich and rare.
Threads of color, bold and bright,
Guide us gently through the night.

With each stitch, a tale unfolds,
Of ancient wisdom and of gold.
We spin our yarns with joyful mirth,
In the fabric of our shared Earth.

So let us thread our thoughts anew,
Together, crafting something true.
In this loom of life we stand,
Creating beauty, hand in hand.

Enchanted Collaborations

Under moonlight, dreams align,
Hearts and minds in perfect rhyme.
Crafted moments, pure and rare,
In enchanted spaces, we prepare.

Voices blend in harmony,
Creating magic, wild and free.
Each word a spark, each laugh a song,
In this union, we all belong.

Together we can paint the skies,
With colors born of heartfelt ties.
Collaboration's gentle art,
Brings forth beauty from the heart.

With every breath, we build a world,
Where joy and wonder are unfurled.
In the dance of shared intent,
Ephemeral gifts are heaven-sent.

So let us gather, hand in hand,
To work together, understand.
In this embrace, our spirits glide,
Enchanted journeys, side by side.

The Conflux of Ideas

A river flows where thoughts converge,
Ideas spark, and visions surge.
In the current, we find our way,
Navigating night and day.

Minds collide with vibrant grace,
In this vast and open space.
Each connection fuels the fire,
A symphony of rich desire.

With open hearts, we share a breath,
Transcending borders, life and death.
The fusion of our dreams is bright,
As we illuminate the night.

From chaos blooms the sweetest chance,
In the dance of a cosmic trance.
Threads of reason intertwine,
Creating brilliance, so divine.

Let's celebrate this wondrous tide,
Where no thought alone must abide.
In the conflux, we find the way,
To forge a brighter, shared today.

Shaped by Shadows

In twilight's grasp, we find our fears,
Casting shadows, formed by tears.
Yet in the dark, the light reveals,
The power that our spirit seals.

We learn to dance within the gloom,
Embracing forms that softly bloom.
Each shadow tells a tale of change,
In stillness, life can feel so strange.

Through every darkened path we tread,
A symphony of hope is spread.
Shaped by shadows, we arise,
Transforming pain into the skies.

Light and dark, they intertwine,
A tapestry of the divine.
In every shadow, a spark may lie,
Illuminating all we try.

So let us walk with courage bold,
In the darkness, stories told.
For every shadow bears a light,
Guiding us through endless night.

Blended Canvases

Colors dance in gentle sway,
Brushstrokes whisper secrets bold.
Canvas worlds where night meets day,
Imagination's tales unfold.

A splash of light, a touch of dark,
Textures weave a vibrant scene.
In every line, there's a spark,
Visions float where dreams convene.

Shapes collide, they twist and twine,
Harmony in chaos found.
In this blend, we intertwine,
Beauty roots beneath the ground.

Melodies of color blend,
Layered stories, soft and loud.
With every stroke, our hearts we send,
A canvas speaks when dreams are proud.

Voices in Texture

Hands that shape the silent clay,
Whisper how the world should feel.
Each rough edge and soft array,
Carries truths that gently heal.

Patterns rise from hidden seams,
Threaded tales of life and love.
Ribbons dancing with our dreams,
Textures guide the heart above.

Fingers trace the paths of time,
Echos linger in the air.
Every fold, a subtle rhyme,
Voices weave a tapestry rare.

In the shadows, stories bloom,
Sculpting tales both bright and dark.
Every linger, every room,
Holds the whispers, each a spark.

The Fusion of Dreams

Stars collide in midnight's gleam,
Weaving destinies anew.
In the heart, we dare to dream,
Merging worlds with every view.

Thoughts like rivers, flowing free,
Currents twist and turn in flight.
Where the mind and soul agree,
Imagination ignites the night.

Visions rise, a phoenix bold,
From the ashes, hope does shine.
In this fusion, countless fold,
Every heartbeat, a design.

Bridges made from whispered fears,
Connecting realms of light and shade.
Together we can shed our tears,
Crafting dreams that never fade.

Fractured Reflections

Mirrors break, but never lie,
Shards reveal what's deep inside.
In their pieces, truths can fly,
Facing fears, we do not hide.

Light refracts in colors bright,
Playing on the cracks of glass.
In this maze lies pure insight,
Finding peace as moments pass.

Jumbled images align,
In the chaos, beauty thrives.
From the fragments, we define,
Life's mosaic, how it strives.

Each reflection bears a story,
Layers woven in our skin.
Through the dark and into glory,
Fractured paths lead us within.

Weaving Worlds Together

Threads of thought intertwine,
In the loom of night and day.
Each vision a spark divine,
Together we shape the way.

Hands unite in gentle grace,
Crafting dreams from whispered sighs.
In this vast and sacred space,
Hope ascends as the heart flies.

Colors blend, the shadows dance,
We find strength in unity.
In each weave, there's a chance,
To embrace our shared journey.

Echoes of laughter and song,
Filling the tapestry's seam.
In this world where we belong,
We gather threads of a dream.

Bridges built from heart to heart,
Creating bonds, we find the light.
In this weave, we play our part,
Together, we ignite the night.

Breathing Life into Color

A brush strokes the canvas bright,
With each hue, a story grows.
In the dance of day and night,
Art awakens, boldly glows.

Whispers of nature's embrace,
Paint the world with tender care.
Every shade holds a warm trace,
Of the joy we all can share.

Splash of red, a spark of fire,
Blue like oceans deep and wide.
In this palette, we conspire,
To paint the heart's gentle pride.

Through each stroke, we find our way,
Resonating with the soul.
In the colors, we can stay,
Life's a canvas, rich and whole.

Breathe it in, the vivid light,
Let it flow like rivers free.
In this spectrum, take your flight,
Color brings us harmony.

Spirit of the Collective

Voices rise, a symphony,
Echoes of hearts intertwined.
In this circle, we shall be,
A force of love, unconfined.

Hands held tight, a shared embrace,
In the warmth of kindred souls.
Together we find our place,
Filled with dreams that make us whole.

From each story, strength we gain,
In the tapestry of life.
Through the joy and through the pain,
We unite to end the strife.

Life's a dance, a sacred flow,
Rhythms of hope, pulse in time.
With each step, we come to know,
We are one, a painted rhyme.

Lift your voice, let's raise it high,
In the spirit, we will shine.
Through the laughter, hear the cry,
Together, we are the divine.

The Fluidity of Form

Water flows with grace untamed,
Challenging the paths it takes.
In its dance, there's beauty claimed,
Life's a river that awakes.

Mountain peaks and valleys deep,
All the shapes we can explore.
In the silence, secrets seep,
As we seek what's at the core.

Life's a canvas, constantly,
Shifting with the tides of time.
In the change, we come to see,
Every moment, a new rhyme.

Breathe in deeply, let it show,
Embrace the ebb and the flow.
In this dance, we come to know,
We are part of the great glow.

Fleeting forms that shape the night,
Stars that twinkle, fade, and bloom.
In the fluid, find the light,
Life's a song, dispelling doom.

Colorful Tapestries of Thought

In shades of dreams, ideas swirl,
A vivid dance, each thought a pearl.
Through vibrant hues, reflections gaze,
Unraveling secrets in painted maze.

Brush strokes speak, a tale to tell,
In every color, emotions swell.
From dark to light, the journey flows,
A world of wonders, it brightly glows.

The canvas whispers, stories blend,
A tapestry woven, art won't end.
Imagined realms where visions play,
In a burst of colors, thoughts convey.

Each layer depth, a voice, a sound,
Where silence lingers, magic found.
A living poem, rich and grand,
In colorful tapestries, we stand.

Let us explore, our minds set free,
In every hue, a memory.
The art of thought, profound and wide,
In colorful realms, we take our stride.

Harmonies in Canvas

With every stroke, a note does rise,
The canvas hums, beneath the skies.
Colors intermingle, a song in light,
Harmonies dance, day turns to night.

Blues and greens in laughter blend,
Each hue a harmony, soft to mend.
Yellows beam like sunlit songs,
In the symphony where art belongs.

Textures weave a fabric true,
Silent rhythms, both old and new.
Against the canvas, emotions thrive,
In vibrant ties, our spirits dive.

Every corner, a melody clear,
Painting whispers that we can hear.
In swirls of passion, creation flows,
A harmony that forever grows.

Let hearts collide in this embrace,
Through brush and color, find our place.
In every canvas, life takes wing,
To the harmony of the heart we sing.

Whispers of Brush and Tone

A brush upon the canvas glides,
Whispers chase where silence hides.
Tone and shade in soft caress,
In every stroke, emotions press.

Gentle colors blend and sway,
Stories hidden, come out to play.
From softest pastels to deep, bold shades,
A world of wonders, where light cascades.

With every line, a tale unfolds,
Of dreams and fears, of hearts that hold.
In layers thick, a mystery grows,
In the whispers of tone, the heart knows.

Let shadows linger, let echoes ring,
In the dance of color, life takes wing.
Each brush's touch, a sweet refrain,
In whispers of art, we break the chain.

A canvas breathes, alive and free,
Through whispers gathered, we can see.
In every tone, a heartbeat found,
In art's embrace, we are unbound.

Symphony of the Senses

A symphony blooms, colors collide,
In every note, emotions abide.
The heartbeat of art, a sweet refrain,
In the dance of senses, joy and pain.

Visual splendor meets the ear,
In hues that dance, the heart draws near.
A fragrant breeze on a sunny day,
In this orchestra, we find our way.

Textures linger, touch inspires,
Warmth of colors, igniting fires.
In flavors rich and tales of old,
The symphony's story is beautifully told.

Feel the rhythm, time slows down,
In every stroke, wear art's crown.
In the blending of senses, we reside,
In a symphony vast, our hearts open wide.

As melodies weave through the day,
In art's embrace, we find our way.
A vibrant world that sings and sways,
In the symphony of life, love plays.

Sculpting Silence into Sound

In whispers soft, the echoes rise,
Crafted notes, a gentle guise.
Each breath a brush, each pause a hue,
Shaping worlds with every cue.

Wood and wind, in harmony blend,
A silent space where dreams ascend.
Melodies dance on fading light,
In stillness born, the songs ignite.

Through trembling strings, emotions weave,
A tapestry that we believe.
Layers of echoes, rich and bold,
In silence deep, the tale unfolds.

From quiet realms, the sound is drawn,
Painting twilight, dusk to dawn.
Euphony's kiss, a fleeting chance,
As heartbeats join in muted dance.

With every chord, a universe,
Sculpting silence, art's reverse.
In whispered tone, the night unwinds,
Into a song, the silence blinds.

Fragments of Reality Colliding

Shards of truth in chaotic flight,
Dancing shadows in fading light.
A world divided, still it spins,
Where loss and laughter both begin.

Mirrors crack, reflections shatter,
Voices blend, each note a clatter.
Moments clash in vivid hues,
Lost in time, we seek to choose.

Timepieces shiver, seconds stray,
Chasing dreams that slip away.
Reality bends, a fleeting game,
In the fragments, none the same.

Through twisted paths, we wander far,
Guided by a distant star.
Colliding worlds, a fierce embrace,
In the chaos, we find our place.

Each discarded piece, a thread we weave,
Binding stories we can't conceive.
As fragments merge, a vision grows,
In collisions deep, the mystery flows.

The Mosaic of Hidden Visions

Tiny pieces, colors bright,
A mosaic crafted from lost light.
In silence found, the fragments sing,
A hidden world that dreams can bring.

Each shard a story, whispered past,
Moments captured, echoes cast.
Shapes of longing, woven tight,
In every angle, shadows bite.

Layers deep, the vision hides,
Behind the mask, the truth abides.
Unraveling threads of life unseen,
In broken seams, the soul intervenes.

With every touch, creation flows,
The mosaic glimmers, brightly glows.
Artistry born from pain and grace,
Each hidden vision finds its place.

In vibrant chaos, life stands still,
As pieces fall to shape the will.
A dance of colors, stories unfold,
In the mosaic, we are bold.

Enchantments of Mixed Mediums

Paint and paper, clay in hand,
Crafting dreams, where wishes stand.
Textures merge, a tapestry spun,
With every layer, we become one.

Ink flows freely, whispers wear,
Capturing thoughts that linger there.
Sculpted forms, in stillness wait,
Expressions bloom, we navigate.

Collage of colors, rich and wild,
Unruly beauty, the muse's child.
Each stroke a heartbeat, rhythms blend,
In mixed mediums, we transcend.

From charcoal lines to brushy strokes,
Every failure, a token provokes.
In this realm, the limits break,
Art as life, our souls awake.

Through binding threads and woven fates,
Enchantments rise as passion creates.
In every medium, love abounds,
In mixed forms, the heart resounds.

A Symphony of Senses

In twilight's calm embrace, a whisper calls,
The scent of jasmine dances in the night.
Fingers brush the petals, soft as silk,
A melody unnotes, waiting for light.

Beneath the moon's gaze, secrets unfold,
The taste of summer lingers on the tongue.
Crickets harmonize in silver tones,
Nature's choir sings, eternally young.

Echoes of laughter float through the trees,
Each rustle of leaves is a soft refrain.
A cool breeze wraps around like a cloak,
Enveloping dreams in a delicate chain.

In the distance, a river flows and sighs,
Its voice, a gentle hush, whispers to me.
The warmth of sunlight breaks dawn's quiet calm,
Awakening all in a sacred decree.

A symphony of senses, all entwined,
United in nature's grand, sweet embrace.
In this moment, every heartbeat aligns,
Life's brief sonnet, rapture we chase.

The Failures of Colors

Red screams with passion, but bleeds into shame,
While blue whispers loneliness under the moon.
Yellow's bright laughter fades into despair,
As joy evaporates far too soon.

Green holds the promise of life yet to thrive,
Yet withers in shadows of winter's cold hand.
Orange ignites dreams with flickers of hope,
But flickers then falter, no longer can stand.

Purple's deep mystique may captivate heart,
Yet hides in illusions of grandeur's tight grip.
A spectrum of stories, all begging for grace,
In the canvas of life, the colors all slip.

The failures of colors collide in a dance,
Each hue, a reflection of joy and of strife.
With brushes of fate, they paint true and false,
As chaos and beauty twirl in this life.

In a world where shadows eclipse the bright light,
We search for the shades that reveal what we crave.
Though the palette may falter, it's here we find hope,
In the failures of colors, our spirits can save.

Narratives in Neons

Neon lights flicker, painting the streets,
Stories emerge in the dark night air.
Glowing signs beckon with promises bold,
Each corner alive with a tale to share.

Amidst the shadows, whispers resound,
Footsteps echo in rhythms of dreams.
City pulse thumps with electric delight,
As life weaves together in vibrant seams.

Through smoky bars and crowded cafes,
Voices collide in a cacophonous roar.
Old souls and strangers intertwine their paths,
A tapestry woven forevermore.

Lime and fuchsia blend into the night,
Creating a canvas of laughter and sighs.
In hues so vivid, the heart finds its beat,
In narratives woven, where laughter never dies.

Chasing the glow, we wander and roam,
In this neon jungle, dreams dance and sway.
Through vivid hues, we seek our own stories,
In the city's embrace, we find our own way.

Choreography of Color and Light

Brush strokes dance with vibrant hue,
Shadows twirl in the morning dew.
Canvas breathes with every shade,
A symphony of light displayed.

Colors blend, a fluid play,
Whispers of dawn, brightening the day.
Each hue speaks of joy and grace,
Crafting beauty in every space.

From twilight's kiss to starry night,
Every glance ignites pure delight.
Framed in stillness, stories flow,
In waves of color, emotions grow.

Choreographed by unseen hands,
Painted dreams from distant lands.
A vivid world takes its flight,
Living art, eternal light.

Together, they weave a tale,
In a dance where none can fail.
Brushes flutter, spirits soar,
In this ballet, forevermore.

Fusions of Rhythm and Texture

The drumbeat calls in the dark night,
Echoes of passion, pure delight.
Strings entwine, a soft embrace,
As melodies carve their sacred space.

Fingers glide on supple skin,
Layers weave where dreams begin.
The heartbeat quickens, souls awake,
In every note, the rhythms break.

Textures blend in a warm embrace,
Creating art in time and space.
The world sways to the gentle sound,
As harmony in motion is found.

Dancers move through vibrant air,
Spirits lift in the music's care.
With every beat, we come alive,
In this moment, together we strive.

In fusions deep, our hearts align,
Threads of life in design divine.
United in sound, we rise and flow,
In this tapestry, love will grow.

Echoes of the Unseen Hand

Whispers curl in the evening air,
Unseen paths lead us unaware.
Gentle nudges, the mind's delight,
Guiding fate through shadowy night.

Ink flows softly on the page,
Stories dance, transcending age.
Beneath the surface, secrets hide,
In every heartbeat, dreams confide.

The brush strokes all feel like fate,
Creating worlds, we contemplate.
With every flick and every twist,
The unseen hand we can't resist.

Voices linger in tales untold,
Of moments captured, hearts of gold.
In silence speaks the artist's plea,
Echoes of what we cannot see.

Through time we wander, woven tight,
In echoes soft, we find the light.
A tapestry rich and diverse,
The unseen hand, our universe.

The Alchemy of Creative Minds

In the cauldron of thought, dreams ignite,
Turning chaos to form, day to night.
Ideas mingle, collide, and fuse,
Crafting wonders we dare not refuse.

Words create a magic unbound,
Resonating through silence profound.
With every stroke, the mind reveals,
The essence of what the spirit feels.

From the heart, the universe flows,
Alchemy hidden in art that grows.
Transformations spark with each new quest,
In a dance of creation, we find rest.

Visionaries weave the fabric of fate,
In the crucible, they contemplate.
With every spark, a journey starts,
Uniting the world, connecting hearts.

The alchemy thrives, a wondrous chain,
Turning love and loss into gain.
Together we craft, with passion and rhyme,
In the alchemy of creative minds.

Canvas of Convergence

On the canvas, dreams collide,
Brushes trace where worlds abide.
Colors merge in whispered tones,
Creating pathways, not alone.

Here the past and future meet,
Every stroke a heartbeat sweet.
Layers blend, a story told,
In vibrant hues, the visions bold.

Underneath the artist's eye,
Visions dance, and passions fly.
A tapestry of thought unfolds,
In every corner, life beholds.

As shadows dance, and light must play,
Truth and beauty find their way.
In the silence, whispers sing,
Of hope and love, eternal spring.

Within this frame, emotions stir,
A harmony of shades, a blur.
Each line, a path to explore,
In the canvas, we crave for more.

Harmonies in Color

Colors burst like laughter bright,
Dancing rhythms, pure delight.
Melodies woven in each hue,
A symphony of lives anew.

Gentle strokes ignite the page,
Each hue a story, age to age.
The canvas hums with joy and pain,
In every shade, the heart's refrain.

From deep crimson to softest blue,
Each blends in harmony, en route.
A chorus of dreams paints the air,
In silent notes, love's gentle care.

In every corner, shadows play,
While sunlight chases clouds away.
These harmonies in colors blend,
A masterpiece that finds no end.

Together here, we sing as one,
In the dance of shade and sun.
Each color speaks of hopes untold,
In harmonies, our hearts unfold.

Interwoven Expressions

Threads of thought in vibrant dance,
Weaving tales of fate and chance.
In textures rich, the stories thrive,
Interwoven, we come alive.

Every fiber holds a dream,
A tapestry where voices beam.
Colors speaking, limbs entwined,
Expressions bold, through hearts aligned.

Gentle whispers of the past,
In every stitch, a bond held fast.
Moments captured, time's embrace,
In woven art, we find our place.

With every thread, a life is spun,
Curated care, the work begun.
Through ups and downs, the patterns show,
In interwoven hearts, we grow.

Together here on this grand loom,
In vibrant shades, we blossom, bloom.
Expressions deep, a world that sings,
Through art's embrace, our freedom brings.

Symphonic Strokes

With every stroke, the canvas breathes,
A symphony of whispered leaves.
Colors swirl in rhythmic flow,
Capturing light, a vibrant glow.

Brushes dance like violin strings,
Creating worlds where beauty clings.
Beneath the chaos, order flows,
In symphonic strokes, the heart knows.

From gentle pastels to bold charades,
Music of color, the soul cascades.
In harmony, each stroke aligns,
A picture painted, love defines.

As symphonies play through thick and fine,
The art reveals a tale divine.
In every splash, a note set free,
Symphonic strokes, our melody.

In this blend, we find our sound,
An orchestra where dreams abound.
Through each canvas, we compose,
In symphonic strokes, the heart exposed.

Sonic Silhouettes

In twilight's glow, whispers entwine,
Melodies drift, a thread divine.
Rhythms pulse, shadows sway,
Echoes of sound, lead the way.

Notes cascade, like raindrops fall,
Harmonies rise, suspending all.
In the silence, secrets blend,
As echoes of night never end.

Voices merge in timeless flight,
Each sonic wave a guiding light.
Silhouettes dance, a vibrant sea,
Together they sing, wild and free.

In this realm, feel the embrace,
Vibrations linger, leaving trace.
Within each note, a dream takes form,
Sonic silhouettes, endlessly warm.

As dusk descends, the world ignites,
With melodies sweet, into the nights.
An orchestra spun from wishes bright,
In the dance of sound, the souls unite.

Where Mediums Meet

Brush strokes linger on canvas bare,
Colors collide, igniting air.
Sculptures rise, form takes flight,
Crafting dreams in morning light.

Words weave tales in spaces wide,
Narratives breath, with hearts they bide.
Fingers plot the course of fate,
Where mediums blend, create, relate.

Photography captures the fleeting day,
Moments preserved in a silent play.
Echoes of memories, soft and sweet,
At the crossroads, where mediums meet.

Dance in motion, a fleeting grace,
Life expressed, in time and space.
Harmony thrives in blended art,
A synthesis bound, heart to heart.

Each stroke a whisper, each word a song,
In this collaboration, we all belong.
Unity found in every form,
Where mediums meet, our spirits warm.

The Language of Light

Golden rays through branches peek,
Illuminating paths we seek.
A dance of shadows; soft and bright,
In every glimmer, whispers ignite.

In twilight hues, dreams take flight,
Colors mingle in fading light.
A spectrum's kiss on nature's face,
The language of light, a soft embrace.

Stars twinkle secrets, celestial scrolls,
Speaking to hearts, connecting souls.
In the dark, each glint unfolds,
Stories of life, in silence told.

Moonbeams bathe in silver grace,
Casting hope in every space.
Through luminous paths, we find our way,
In the language of light, night turns to day.

The sun ignites a fiery hue,
Painting horizons, fresh and new.
Where shadows fade at dawn's first sight,
We learn to speak the language of light.

Erasing Divisions

Between the lines, we start to see,
Threads of connection, you and me.
In shared laughter, we find a way,
Erasing divisions, come what may.

Walls once stood, now gently fade,
With every step, new bridges made.
Unity blooms in hearts and minds,
In kindness shared, compassion finds.

Through whispered tales and glances bright,
We break the silence, embrace the light.
Differences dissolve, as voices blend,
In this harmony, wounds may mend.

Hands held high, together we stand,
A tapestry woven, strand by strand.
Celebrating all, both near and far,
In the dance of love, there lies the star.

So let us speak with actions bold,
Stories of unity waiting to unfold.
Erasing divisions, side by side,
In a world anew, we will abide.

Dances at the Intersection

Beneath the city's flickering lights,
We find a space where shadows blend.
With every step, a story ignites,
In crowded streets, where strangers mend.

Voices rise in a vibrant hum,
Echoing dreams of days gone by.
Hearts beat fast as the night becomes,
A stage for hope, where spirits fly.

Colors clash like works of art,
Painting moments that weave and sway.
Each twirl and spin, a brand new start,
In this mosaic, we find our way.

With every hand that brushes near,
A spark ignites, a bond is made.
Together in rhythm, we conquer fear,
In this dance of life, we are unafraid.

As the night fades to dawn's embrace,
We leave behind the echoes of song.
In memory's heart, we find our place,
Where every dance writes us along.

Patterns Emerging from Chaos

In the whirlwind of thoughts that swirl,
Chaos dances, a sudden flare.
Amidst the noise, new shapes unfurl,
Whispers of truth in the tangled air.

Fractured moments land like rain,
Filling voids, we make our art.
From scattered pieces, joy and pain,
Patterns emerge, each playing a part.

Like fractals forming in the light,
Chaos holds secrets, yet to find.
In the disorder, we gain our sight,
A tapestry woven, our fates entwined.

Through a lens of love, we discern,
Threads of connection in the strife.
In every twist, a lesson to learn,
Beauty blooms from the edges of life.

What seems random can take flight,
With grace hidden in the untamed.
From fragments lost, we gain our might,
Writing our stories, unashamed.

Celebrating Union of Touch and Tone

Hands meet softly, a gentle brush,
In silence, a language of their own.
With each note, a pulse, a rush,
Together they sing, no need for a throne.

Voices intertwine in a melodic trance,
Resonating echoes of hearts aligned.
In every glance, a shared romance,
Unified rhythms, two souls combined.

The warmth of contact, a soothing balm,
Each heartbeat guides the dancers' flow.
In this embrace, the world feels calm,
Where love resides, and laughter grows.

Fingers explore like whispers on skin,
Striking chords that reverberate wide.
Together they meld, like dusk and din,
In this tapestry, we take great pride.

As melodies rise, the night enfolds,
In harmony, they find their way home.
Through touch and tone, a story unfolds,
Celebrating love, wherever they roam.

The Rhythms of Interwoven Lives

In fields where destinies intertwine,
Life's tapestry spins day by day.
Every heartbeat a sacred sign,
In the lore of souls at play.

Footsteps echo in shared spaces,
Guided by fate's careful hand.
In laughter and trials, we find traces,
Of bonds that time will never strand.

From whispered secrets beneath the stars,
To the sunrise that wakes us anew,
In joy and sorrow, we bear our scars,
As life weaves its fabric in hues.

With every choice, the threads we choose,
Create a dance both bold and true.
In unity's heart, we cannot lose,
For together, we shape the view.

As seasons shift and stories blend,
We cherish the paths we walk together.
In the rhythms of life, we transcend,
Connected by dreams, now and forever.

Merging Visions

In twilight's gleam, two paths align,
With whispers soft, they start to twine.
A dance of dreams, where hopes reside,
In colors bold, our worlds collide.

A tapestry, woven tight,
Flecks of gold in fading light.
Each thread a story, old and new,
A canvas vast, in shades of blue.

With every step, our hearts will beat,
In syncopation, fierce and sweet.
Together firm, we craft our fate,
In unity, we navigate.

Through storms that rage, and calm that glows,
We'll stand as one, as friendship grows.
For in this space, our visions clear,
Merging souls, we draw near.

So let us paint with broad strokes bold,
A future bright, with tales retold.
In every hue, in every line,
Our merging visions brightly shine.

The Alchemy of Form

In whispered words, creation brews,
A blend of thoughts, a spark ensues.
From chaos born, new shapes take flight,
In shadows deep, we find the light.

A sculptor's hand, a painter's muse,
Transforming dreams, with vibrant hues.
Each line a pulse, each curve a sigh,
The alchemy of form draws nigh.

An echo lives in marble's grace,
In every contour, storied space.
With gentle touch, we carve our truth,
In fleeting moments, we find our youth.

With eyes wide open, we explore,
The magic hidden at the core.
In every piece a piece of soul,
The alchemy of form makes whole.

So gather round, and let us weave,
In every shape, our heart believe.
Through art, we find what once was lost,
The alchemy of form, at any cost.

Radiant Reimaginings

In daylight's glow, we shift and sway,
Unfolding dreams in bold array.
With every breath, a vision's born,
From faded past, new paths are worn.

Each star above, a thought takes flight,
In radiant fire, we find the light.
A canvas bright with stories told,
In colors rich, a sight to behold.

Through laughter shared and tears that fall,
We gather strength, we rise, we call.
In every heart, a spark ignites,
Radiant reimaginings take flight.

So here we stand, with hands outstretched,
Creating worlds, our dreams etched.
With open minds, we plant the seeds,
In radiant visions, we meet our needs.

Together strong, we shape our place,
In every moment, we find grace.
For in our hearts, the light will shine,
Radiant reimaginings, divine.

Collective Craftsmanship

In unity, our hands combine,
A dance of purpose, spirit's sign.
Through crafted work, we find our way,
Collective dreams in bright array.

With every voice, a note we share,
An echo strong, a heartfelt prayer.
Together we weave with threads of gold,
A tapestry of stories told.

Through trials met and joys embraced,
We learn to move with subtle grace.
In every piece, a part we give,
Collective craftsmanship, we live.

From many minds, a vision clear,
In harmony, we conquer fear.
With every step, a bond we forge,
Collective dreams, as hearts converge.

So let us build, with love our guide,
In every challenge, side by side.
Through crafts we lift, and crafts we bind,
Collective craftsmanship, intertwined.

Dissonant Dreams

In shadows deep, the whispers roam,
A symphony of thoughts, far from home.
Fragments collide, a chaotic dance,
In the night's embrace, they take their chance.

Echoes linger, haunting the mind,
A tapestry of visions, intertwined.
Lost in the maze of fractured light,
Navigating dreams that fuel the night.

Silence shattered, a haunting tune,
Beneath the stars, too bright, too soon.
Dissonant chords, like thunder's roar,
Awaken the heart, yearning for more.

Through twisted paths, resilience gleams,
Amid the ruins of broken dreams.
From discord blooms a vibrant spark,
Guiding the way through shadows dark.

In the end, as dawn breaks free,
Harmony found, a sweet decree.
In dissonant dreams, hope takes flight,
A symphony born from the night.

Unified Visions

Together we stand, on common ground,
In the heart of the storm, our voices sound.
A canvas wide, vivid and true,
Unified visions, a vibrant hue.

Minds intertwined, like threads of gold,
Stories shared, in whispers bold.
With every heartbeat, a promise shared,
Building dreams, where none have dared.

In the garden of thoughts, we plant the seed,
Nurturing hope, fulfilling the need.
Hand in hand, we face the day,
Unified visions, lighting the way.

Waves of passion, surging high,
Chasing shadows, beneath the sky.
In each heartbeat, a story starts,
Unified visions, igniting hearts.

As the sun sets, painting the sky,
Together we'll soar, you and I.
In the tapestry of dreams, we find our space,
Unified visions, a warm embrace.

Kinship of Creativity

In the quiet whispers of the night,
Ideas bloom in soft twilight.
With every stroke, a bond designed,
Kinship of creativity, intertwined.

Voices rise in melodic cheer,
Crafting dreams, holding dear.
With colors splashed, our souls ignite,
In the light of creation, pure and bright.

A dance of thoughts, flowing free,
United in art, just you and me.
Minds in sync, a beautiful trance,
In this kinship, we take our chance.

Stories woven, like threads in cloth,
Moments captured, no need for sloth.
In shared laughter, and tears that gleam,
Kinship of creativity, a wondrous dream.

As the dawn breaks, new worlds emerge,
In this bond, our spirits surge.
Together we sketch, together we play,
Kinship of creativity, guiding our way.

The Pulse of Potential

Beneath the surface, rhythms flow,
A heartbeat strong, waiting to grow.
In the silence, dreams take flight,
The pulse of potential, burning bright.

With every step, a story unfolds,
Unwritten tales of the brave and bold.
In moments fleeting, futures gleam,
The pulse of potential, a shared dream.

Voices echo in the vast expanse,
Calling forth courage, a daring chance.
In unity, we rise and strive,
Embracing the spark that keeps us alive.

Through trials faced, and battles won,
The pulse of potential never done.
In the tapestry of hope, threads align,
Creating a vision, purely divine.

As we journey forth, hand in hand,
Guided by dreams, together we stand.
With faith in our hearts, we break the mold,
The pulse of potential, a story told.

Sketches from the Edge of Reality

Lines blur between day and night,
Shadows dance, taking flight.
Whispers echo in the air,
Fleeting moments, sharp and rare.

Brushstrokes paint a hidden dream,
Fragments of a silent scream.
Canvas stretching into thought,
Elusive truths, dearly sought.

Colors merge in chaotic flow,
Unseen tales, they come and go.
Reality bends, softly sways,
In the quiet, a voice stays.

Glimmers of an other place,
Time dissolves, leaves no trace.
Visions collide, hearts ignite,
In this realm, we find our light.

Echoes linger, shadows twine,
Dreams unfold, perfectly align.
From the edge, we leap and soar,
Sketches drawn, forevermore.

The Fusion of Past and Present

Time weaves through moments past,
Echoes of a love that lasts.
Faded pictures in our minds,
Stories linked, the heart unwinds.

Footsteps traced on ancient ground,
In every story, wisdom found.
Present pulses with the old,
Gold and silver threads are rolled.

Fragments cherished, shards of light,
Guiding us into the night.
In the now, the past will hum,
Together, we will overcome.

Every heartbeat is a song,
In this dance, we all belong.
Living echoes, alive and clear,
In our fusion, we hold dear.

Time's embrace, a gentle touch,
Past and present, woven such.
In every glance, a world appears,
Stories told throughout the years.

Whirlwinds of Vision and Sound

In the storm of thoughts that churn,
Visions flicker, lessons learn.
Melodies in the whirlwinds play,
Crafting magic in the fray.

Notes cascade like raindrops fall,
Echoes rise, we heed the call.
Colors spin in a vibrant dance,
Opening the heart to chance.

Cacophony of dreams unfurled,
A symphony lights up the world.
Whispers swirl like autumn leaves,
In their patterns, the spirit believes.

From chaos blooms a radiant grace,
Every sound holds its own place.
In this whirlwind, we find our ground,
Magic lives in every sound.

Vision bursts like bright confetti,
Moments blend, ever ready.
In heartbeats, we ride the breeze,
Whirlwinds whisper, never cease.

Woven Tales in Every Stroke

Each brush creates, a tale we weave,
In the colors, we believe.
Gentle strokes, like whispers flow,
Stories from the heart we sow.

Textures rich, emotions bare,
With each layer, we lay bare.
In silence, colors start to sing,
Embracing what the canvas brings.

Woven threads of joy and pain,
In each fold, there's much to gain.
Memories captured, life's design,
In every flick, our souls align.

Fingers dance across the page,
Inspiration sparks, we engage.
A tapestry of dreams unfurled,
With every stroke, we shape our world.

Stories linger, timeless grace,
In every stroke, we find our place.
Woven tales from heart to art,
In every piece, a hidden heart.

Unearthing Melodies in Motion

In whispers soft, the music starts,
Each note a pulse, each beat it imparts.
Waves of sound, they rise and fall,
Like breathless waves that heed the call.

Through the air, where shadows play,
Rhythms chase the light of day.
Steps entwined, a fleeting grace,
With every spin, a warm embrace.

In twilight's glow, the echoes blend,
Every story, a message to send.
From silent roots, their voices grow,
A symphony of life, soft and low.

Hearts aligned in a sacred dance,
As melodies weave their sweet romance.
Beneath the stars, in unity,
Unraveled threads of harmony.

Now the evening gently sighs,
As whispers turn to lullabies.
In motion's embrace, we find the key,
To unearth the dreams that long to be.

Merging the Palette of Dreams

Brush in hand, we splash the hues,
Colors blend, ignite the muse.
In every stroke, a thought is born,
From chaos bright, new worlds are sworn.

Crimson skies and emerald seas,
In the canvas, breathe like trees.
Textures form and shadows play,
A vivid dance that drifts away.

Fragments of hope, in every shade,
Through layers deep, the fears now fade.
Each stroke a step in twilight's gleam,
Merging visions, we weave the dream.

A heartbeat echoes on the page,
With every hue, we break the cage.
Together drawn, the colors sway,
As palettes dance in bright array.

Now the picture starts to sing,
In the stillness, joy takes wing.
From dreams we've dared to let unfold,
Art becomes the tales retold.

The Dance of Forms and Shades

Shapes entwined in graceful flow,
Figures rise and start to glow.
In shadows cast, reflections chase,
A vibrant spiral, warm embrace.

Lines that curve and angles meet,
In silent rhythms, hearts will beat.
With every step, the visions swirl,
A dance where light and dark unfurl.

Embracing edges, soft yet bold,
Mysteries in each shape unfold.
Textures whisper, tales of old,
While in the movement, dreams take hold.

Entranced by the spirit of the night,
Forms collide, igniting light.
Through space and time, we intertwine,
To lose ourselves in forms divine.

As final notes in silence spin,
A canvas vast, the dance begins.
With every turn, we weave and sway,
In forms and shades, we find our way.

Threads of Imagination Interwoven

In tapestry of minds we weave,
Every thread a dream to believe.
Colors bright and shadows deep,
Stories shared, in silence we keep.

Memories float on gentle strands,
Entangled hopes held in our hands.
With each pull, a vision blooms,
In the heart, where wonder looms.

Tales connected through the years,
In laughter shared, in hidden tears.
Each pattern tells of love and loss,
Within the weave, we bear the cross.

Hand in hand, we stitch our fate,
Through every twist, new paths create.
In vibrant hues, our dreams are spun,
An endless dance, just begun.

When threads unite, the fabric grows,
In every knot, a life that flows.
Together we weave, forever free,
In threads of imagination, we see.

The Orchestra of Unconventional Forms

In shadows where the colors blend,
A melody of shapes ascend.
Each note a brush, each chord a hue,
The canvas sings, a vibrant view.

The strings, they dance, the brass ignites,
Rhythms pulse through starry nights.
A symphony of voices rise,
From whispered dreams to painted skies.

The drumming heart, a thunder's call,
Echoes softly within us all.
Crescendo builds, yet still we find,
The silence speaks to heart and mind.

Uncertain paths, yet boldly tread,
In notes unscripted, souls are led.
Together in this vibrant throng,
We find the place where we belong.

A world transformed in art's embrace,
In every form, we find our place.
The orchestra, a tapestry,
Of unconventional harmony.

Sculpted Stories in Motion

From marble dreams, the figures rise,
Each curve a whisper, every sigh.
Their stories etched in stone so grand,
In motion captured, dreams still stand.

The hands that shape, the hearts that lead,
In every twist, a tale we heed.
With chisel sharp, they carve the past,
In every form, the shadows cast.

Life breathed in clay, a vibrant mold,
A journey told, both brave and bold.
In every fold, a lesson learned,
Through sculpted tales, our spirits burned.

The dance of light on surfaces bare,
Illuminates the art laid there.
A moment caught, in time confined,
In sculptures still, our lives entwined.

Stories move in silent grace,
A timeless bond we can't erase.
Through sculpted tales, we see the truth,
In motion lies the spark of youth.

Visions from the Heart of Creation

In stillness deep, creation breathes,
Visions rise like autumn leaves.
A flicker born from dreams untold,
In colors bright, the world unfolds.

Through whispered hopes, the canvas glows,
With every line, the passion shows.
From heart to hand, the vision flows,
In every stroke, the spirit grows.

The light of dawn, a painter's muse,
Awakens visions we can't refuse.
In shadows cast, in brightness played,
A tapestry of dreams conveyed.

Within each hue, a story lies,
A glimpse of life through painted skies.
In every frame, emotions flare,
From quiet thought to vibrant air.

Creation's pulse, a rhythm sweet,
In visions grand, our souls compete.
Through every heart's desired aim,
The art we make will stay the same.

Threads of Life Bound in Art

Each thread a tale, unique and fine,
Bound together, lives entwine.
In fabric rich, the stories weave,
Through artful stitches, we believe.

From vibrant hues to textures deep,
The fabric of our dreams we keep.
In every knot, a journey shared,
In threads of life, we are declared.

A tapestry, both bold and bright,
Illuminates the darkest night.
With every loop, our hopes connect,
In woven tales, we find respect.

Through art, the past and present sway,
In every piece, our voices play.
A culture rich, a history penned,
In threads of life, we comprehend.

Each woven strand, a bond so true,
In art we find the strength to renew.
Together here, we share our part,
In every thread, the beating heart.

Montage of the Soul

In silence whispers thoughts arise,
Fragments dance beyond the skies.
Layered hues of joy and pain,
Each moment etched like gentle rain.

Dreams like shadows softly play,
Guiding hearts along the way.
Every heartbeat tells a tale,
Of battles fought, and dreams that sail.

In mirrored depths, reflections gleam,
Weaving through the fabric of a dream.
A tapestry of hope we weave,
In every breath, we learn to believe.

Ebbing tides of years gone by,
Shapes our spirit, reaching high.
In every echo, we find grace,
A montage of the soul's embrace.

Bound by love, set free by light,
Guided gently through the night.
Each memory, a vibrant thread,
In this tapestry, we are led.

Colors Beyond Boundaries

Brushstrokes blend in vibrant hues,
Whispers of the morning dew.
Each color born from dreams untold,
A canvas bright, a heart of gold.

Beyond the limits, visions soar,
In every shade, we long for more.
Life in colors, wild and free,
Unfurling like a boundless sea.

Crimson passions, azure skies,
Emerald fields where hope lies.
Golden rays through twilight's chill,
An artist's heart, forever will.

Painting visions, bold and true,
Every stroke, a world anew.
In this journey, we embrace,
Colors fill the empty space.

Beyond the limits, love can thrive,
In vivid shades, we learn to strive.
Together, in this grand design,
We find our souls in light divine.

Medley of Marvels

In every breath, a spark ignites,
A symphony of whispered lights.
Notes of laughter blend with sighs,
Creating worlds beyond the skies.

Moments gather, sweet and rare,
A tapestry of love and care.
In fleeting time, we weave our song,
With every note, we all belong.

Miracles in simplest things,
Joy in the song that nature sings.
Glistening stars in velvet night,
A medley of hope, a pure delight.

Colors swirl, and dreams take flight,
Illuminated by the moonlight.
Together in this grand ballet,
We dance our cares and fears away.

Each heartbeat plays a melody,
Resonating, wild and free.
In this symphony, we find,
A world of marvels intertwined.

Interlaced Inspirations

Threads of thought in patterns weave,
Stories shared, and hearts believe.
Interlaced with dreams and fears,
In whispered hopes, we shed our tears.

Ideas bloom like flowers bright,
In the garden of the night.
Together, we create and grow,
In the warmth of love's soft glow.

Moments captured, memories bright,
Shaping shadows into light.
Each inspiration leads the way,
Guiding us through night and day.

A tapestry of minds combined,
In harmony, our hearts aligned.
Interwoven paths we tread,
With every step, new wonders spread.

Through explorations, we ignite,
A spark of vision, bold and bright.
Together, we will find our place,
In interlaced inspirations' grace.

Fusion of Dreams and Canvas

Beneath the twilight's soft embrace,
Colors mingle, leaving no trace.
Whispers of hopes begin to bloom,
Crafting beauty in the gloom.

Each stroke tells a tale anew,
Fleeting moments, bright and true.
Dreams collide in vibrant hues,
Painting life with all we choose.

The brush dances, fluid and free,
Merging visions, you and me.
Layers build, their stories blend,
In this space, where dreams ascend.

Canvas holds our secret schemes,
Woven tightly, yet it seems.
Fusions of what can only be,
A masterpiece for us to see.

Eclipsed by night, we'll find our way,
Colors brightening shades of gray.
Together crafting worlds sublime,
In this fusion, we transcend time.

Palette of Infinite Possibilities

In a palette wide and grand,
Feel the magic in each hand.
Colors blend and softly merge,
Creation stirs within, to urge.

A dash of sun, a hint of night,
Shapes and shadows, pure delight.
From despair to vivid cheer,
Every choice, a path sincere.

Brush in hand, I trace my fate,
Infinite worlds I create.
Every hue a chance to soar,
In this space, forevermore.

Splashes bright and soft, serene,
Palette sings of what has been.
Layers deep, in textures sweet,
Every heartbeat finds its beat.

Imagining what can unfold,
In the colors bright and bold.
Together weaving dreams anew,
In this palette, me and you.

Essence of Creation in Collision

In chaos lies a spark divine,
Creation dances on the line.
Fates entwined in wild embrace,
An essence found in the chase.

Collision brings a new frontier,
Every thought, a voice to hear.
From the ashes, visions rise,
Crafting dreams, igniting skies.

Flares of brilliance in the dark,
Every moment leaves a mark.
Shapes collide, ideas play,
In this dance, we find our way.

Fragments join, a puzzle vast,
Living echoes of the past.
In every clash, potential's born,
Creation thrums, new worlds adorn.

In essence, we begin to see,
All the paths this life can be.
Through collision, we ignite,
A tapestry of dreams in flight.

Sketching the Breath of Inspiration

On the paper, visions flow,
Each mark vibrant, setting glow.
Sketching dreams, the soul's delight,
Breath of art, igniting night.

Gentle strokes, a soft caress,
Whispers of creativity's bless.
Lines entwine in silent song,
In this moment, we belong.

Breath of life in every curve,
Drawing out what we deserve.
Inspiration sparkles bright,
Guiding hearts in endless flight.

With each sketch, we dare to dream,
Finding beauty in the stream.
Creating worlds that intertwine,
In this breath, we taste the divine.

Sketching shadows, bright and bold,
Whispers of stories yet untold.
In every line, a heartbeat's plea,
Inspiration thrives, wild and free.

Melding of Minds

Thoughts like rivers gently flow,
Intertwining in a vibrant glow.
Whispers shared in silent night,
Two hearts dance in shared delight.

Ideas spark, ignite the air,
In unity, we lay ourselves bare.
The tapestry of dreams we weave,
In every thread, we believe.

Minds converge, a brilliant light,
Casting shadows, chasing fright.
Together we break through the mold,
A story of us, forever told.

In conversations deep and true,
We grow beyond just me and you.
The melding of thoughts, pure design,
A masterpiece that is divine.

Through challenges, we stand as one,
An unyielding bond, never done.
In the symphony of thought, we play,
A melody that will not fray.

Echoes of Aesthetic

In colors bright, emotions soar,
Each stroke tells tales of yore.
Brush in hand, the heart takes flight,
Echoes dance in morning light.

Textures blend, like whispers low,
Capturing moments, ebb and flow.
Lines collide on canvas bare,
A dialogue woven with care.

In shapes divine, beauty found,
A symphony of sight, profound.
Artful echoes, deep and wide,
Reflecting worlds we cannot hide.

Through shadows cast and brilliance bright,
We chase the essence of pure delight.
In the gallery of dreams we tread,
Voices linger long after we're dead.

Each masterpiece a timeless song,
In aesthetics, we all belong.
With every hue, each note we sing,
Echoes resonate, forever ring.

United in Brushstrokes

With every stroke, a story starts,
A canvas holds our beating hearts.
Two artists blend in perfect flow,
Creating worlds, letting love show.

Side by side, our visions merge,
In colors bright, our dreams emerge.
Lines entwined, creating space,
A tapestry of time and place.

Brushes dance with tender grace,
In swirling hues, we find our place.
Together we build, with every shade,
In artistry, foundations laid.

As we paint, our spirits soar,
In every layer, we explore.
Each canvas whispers our embrace,
United in this sacred space.

Underneath the artist's sky,
We dream anew, we learn to fly.
In brushstrokes bold, our voices shine,
Creating art, forever divine.

The Song of Fusion

In the silence, a melody calls,
Harmony thrives, as darkness falls.
Voices blend, like night and day,
Creating magic in a new way.

In every note, a heartbeat found,
Lost in rhythm, we're glory-bound.
Together we rise, lyrics entwined,
The song of fusion, truly divine.

Across the void, our spirits meet,
Dance of passion, a rhythmic beat.
Verses flow like rivers anew,
In every measure, something true.

In the chorus, echoes reside,
Celebrating all that we confide.
Notes of laughter, tears unfurl,
Unified in this vibrant whirl.

As we sing under the stars so bright,
A symphony sparkles through the night.
In the fusion of sound, we find our place,
Together in this endless embrace.

Scribbles of Rebellion and Peace

In shadows cast by angry hands,
We draw our lines on shifting sands.
With every stroke, we fight for space,
A canvas shaped by hope and grace.

Our voices rise, a fervent call,
In whispered truths we won't let fall.
We scribble fiercely, bold and bright,
Rebellion dances in the light.

The echo of the streets we roam,
From every heart, we find our home.
With every mark, a tale unfolds,
A spirit fierce, a fire bold.

Yet peace is planted in the fray,
In unity, we find our way.
Above the chaos, dreams take flight,
Through scribbles, we embrace the night.

Together, let our stories blend,
With art as voice, and love, our pen.
We sketch a world that knows no bounds,
In every heart, rebellion sounds.

The Textures of Collective Echoes

In whispers shared, our voices weave,
A tapestry of hopes we believe.
Each sound a thread, entwined and strong,
Together we sing a vibrant song.

From echoes deep, our stories rise,
A chorus born beneath the skies.
Each texture rich, like earth and stone,
In every pulse, we find our own.

The softest sighs, the loudest shouts,
In every heart, a dance that routes.
We trace the lines of joy and pain,
In unity, we learn to gain.

A blend of voices, layered tight,
Transforming shadows into light.
In harmony, we craft the song,
A celebration, bold and strong.

Together we stand, a living art,
With every echo, we impart.
In textures woven, we find peace,
A world transformed, our love's release.

Time Collages in Color

Each moment slips through fingers fast,
A memory captured, shadows cast.
In hues of laughter, shades of tears,
We paint the canvas of our years.

With scattered bits of yesterday,
We weave them into new displays.
In vibrant strokes, both light and dark,
Our tales unfold, ignite a spark.

The past invites the present near,
In every fragment, love and fear.
Colors clash, yet blend anew,
A collage rich in every hue.

Through sunlit days and moonlit nights,
Time dances with its soft delights.
In every glance, a story told,
A quilt of life, both warm and bold.

Embrace the layers, let them shine,
In every crease, a heart divine.
With time collected, we shall grow,
In colors bright, our dreams will flow.

Harmonized Chaos on Display

In wild designs, the heart does thrum,
A symphony of sound and drum.
With edges blurring, lines collide,
In chaos, beauty will not hide.

The dance of thoughts, a frenetic sway,
Unraveling patterns, night and day.
Each note we play, a vibrant clash,
Together blooming, bold and brash.

Colors swirl in rhythmic flow,
As passions burst, our spirits glow.
The art of life, both fierce and free,
In every frame, our unity.

Though chaos reigns, we find our tune,
In broken pieces, we're immune.
With laughter loud and voices strong,
We sketch a world where we belong.

Through harmonized disarray we soar,
Inventing paths unseen before.
In every layer, life's embrace,
Together we find our rightful place.

Chords of Craft

In shadows deep, the craftsmen toil,
Their hands, a dance, on sacred soil.
With wood and string, they weave their sound,
In every note, a story found.

Each strum a heartbeat, each chord a tale,
In harmony, their spirits sail.
From silence born, the music flows,
In every note, the passion grows.

They shape the air, and time stands still,
With gentle grace, they bend to will.
A song emerges, pure and bright,
Illuminating the darkest night.

The rhythm pulses, alive and bold,
In every hand, a piece of gold.
Crafted with love, each line connects,
A tapestry of sound reflects.

With every beat, a world ignites,
A symphony of starry nights.
In chords of craft, our hearts convene,
Creating dreams, both fierce and keen.

Whispers of Unity

In quiet rooms where shadows blend,
A gentle touch, hearts start to mend.
In whispers low, intentions shared,
In every soul, a bond declared.

Through laughter light, and tears once shed,
In every moment, love is spread.
Together strong, we face the fight,
In unity, we claim the light.

With open arms, we stand as one,
Under the watch of the rising sun.
In kindness found, our spirits soar,
In every heart, we learn to trust more.

Each whispered truth, a seed we sow,
A garden rich, where friendships grow.
In harmony, our voices rise,
A chorus vast beneath the skies.

Bound by our dreams, we forge ahead,
With every step, the path we tread.
In whispers soft, we find our way,
United forever, come what may.

Brush and Melody

With colors bright, the canvas calls,
In strokes of joy, the vision sprawls.
A brush in hand, the world awakes,
In every hue, creation shakes.

Melodies dance on air so sweet,
Each note a pulse, each beat a treat.
In art and sound, the soul takes flight,
Creating visions, pure delight.

Mixing shades, a palette rare,
In every splash, we find our care.
A symphony of sight and sound,
In beauty's grasp, the heart is bound.

As colors twine, the rhythms blend,
A masterpiece, no start, no end.
In brush and melody, dreams arise,
A world transformed before our eyes.

Together they weave, both soft and bold,
In every piece, a story told.
In brush and song, we find our call,
In every stroke, we lose it all.

Sculpting Stories

From ancient stone, the figures burst,
A sculptor's hand, both skilled and cursed.
With every chip, a tale takes form,
In quiet strength, the art is born.

With vision clear, the rock reveals,
The depths of life, the truth congeals.
In shadows cast, the stories sigh,
In every curve, a whispered cry.

The hammer strikes, the dust takes flight,
A dance of time, in day and night.
With patience vast, the tale unfolds,
In silent breaths, the heart beholds.

As raw as earth, as soft as air,
In sculpting stories, we lay bare.
Each piece a journey, carved with care,
In every touch, we find what's rare.

From stone to soul, we bridge the gap,
Creating dreams within the gap.
In sculpting stories, we embrace,
The beauty found in every face.

Voices of the Void

In the silence where shadows dwell,
Whispers echo without a bell.
Faint murmurs drift on midnight air,
Carried softly, a ghostly prayer.

Stars like lanterns begin to gleam,
Painting night with a fleeting dream.
Each breath held tight in a chilly dawn,
Life's rhythm plays on, and we move on.

Amongst the stillness, truths arise,
Reflecting hopes in hidden skies.
The void may beckon with haunting grace,
Yet in its depths, we find our place.

A tapestry woven with threads of night,
Every thread a moment, a fleeting light.
In the quiet, we learn to choose,
Embrace the echoes, or face the blues.

So listen close to the silent call,
In the void, there's music that binds us all.
Though shadows dance and echo stray,
Voices of the void will lead the way.

The Curvature of Connection

Beneath the sky, two souls collide,
In the dance of fate, they will abide.
A twist of time, a gentle turn,
In every glance, the embers burn.

Like rivers winding through the land,
Each curve and bend, a touch, a hand.
Moments gathered like scattered seeds,
Together growing from tender needs.

The laughter shared, a vibrant thread,
Interlacing stories, hearts widespread.
In the parables of day to day,
Connections flourish and find their way.

Through stormy weather and skies so blue,
Every challenge faced, they will renew.
Boundless journeys begin in trust,
As dreams entwine, as they must.

With every heartbeat, distance fades,
In the curvature where love cascades.
Two bodies merge, a brilliant spark,
In this connection, they leave their mark.

Shades of One Heart

In the canvas of life, colors blend,
Each shade whispers stories, hearts they send.
The hues of joy and strokes of pain,
Together forming a vibrant chain.

Deep indigos of a long-lost night,
Merge with the yellows that share the light.
Every blend tells a tale anew,
Of laughter shared and skies so blue.

Through every struggle, a palette grows,
Brushes of time, crafting highs and lows.
A symphony painted in shades so bold,
The rhythm of life, a story told.

As seasons shift, the colors flow,
In the warmth, where soft winds blow.
An artist's heart, with strokes of grace,
Finds beauty in every embrace.

In shades of one heart, unity thrives,
Dancing together, where love survives.
Let the colors mingle, forever part,
For in the art, beats a single heart.

Whirlwind of Wisdom

In the tempest of thought, wisdom spins,
Each lesson learned, new chance begins.
A swirling dance of doubt and belief,
Through every trial, we find relief.

Voices of ages whisper through air,
Crafting paths in the midst of despair.
A whirlwind stirs, bringing forth change,
Inviting hearts to rearrange.

In moments of stillness, we listen close,
To echoes of wisdom, we cherish most.
Each spiral of thought leads us to find,
The quiet strength of the open mind.

Through chaos and calm, the journey flows,
Finding solace where the wild wind blows.
In the spiral's embrace, truths unfold,
Lessons of life, timeless and bold.

So let us dance in the midst of the storm,
In the whirlwind of wisdom, we transform.
Each thought a petal, each breath a seed,
In this dance of knowledge, we are freed.

The Fluidity of Expression

Words flow like rivers, wide and deep,
Carving valleys where meanings seep.
Thoughts cascade in vibrant hues,
A dance of language, ever new.

In whispers soft, in shouts so bold,
Stories unfold, waiting to be told.
Emotions ripple, twist and turn,
In the heart of the listener, they burn.

Beneath the surface, currents play,
Hidden meanings find their way.
Expressions shift, like tides at sea,
Unraveling thoughts, setting them free.

Crafting visions with brush and pen,
From fleeting moments, we begin again.
Fluidity binds us, a shared refrain,
In the art of expression, we find no chain.

So let the rivers of voice run clear,
Let creativity rise, let go of fear.
In every stroke, in every sound,
The fluidity of life is found.

Collisions of Idea and Form

Sparks ignite where thought collides,
In the chaos where brilliance hides.
Shapes and colors clash and blend,
Creating worlds where dreams transcend.

Lines intertwine, a dance of fate,
In every conflict, we navigate.
The clash of minds, a vibrant storm,
Emerging visions begin to form.

Conversations bubble, fervent, loud,
In every gathering, we are proud.
From discord rises harmony,
In collisions, we find unity.

Ideas fracture, then reassemble,
In every challenge, our thoughts resemble.
A tapestry woven from threads of light,
In collisions of day and the depth of night.

So let us clash, collide and spark,
In this dance of vision, we leave our mark.
For in strange forms, new truths we find,
Collisions of thought, uniquely combined.

Restless Notes on Canvas

Brush strokes dart like restless dreams,
Across the canvas, bursting seams.
Colors mingle, bright and bold,
In every stroke, a story told.

Melodies weave through the air so fine,
Chasing shadows, drawn by design.
Each note a whisper, each chord a sigh,
Echoing tales of the heart's reply.

Yet stillness calls amid the dance,
In quiet spaces, we find our chance.
To breathe, to ponder, to let creation flow,
In moments of peace, our passions grow.

The canvas breathes, and so do we,
In restless notes, we long to be free.
To capture the fleeting, the fires that burn,
Creating the art of which we learn.

So let us play, let colors scream,
In the restless notes of a vibrant dream.
For on this canvas, we find our place,
A sanctuary where we embrace.

Unfolding Layers of Creation

Peeling back the layers, one by one,
Revealing treasures hidden from the sun.
In every fold, a secret lies,
Awakening wonder, lifting ties.

Crafted moments, stitched with care,
In patterns woven, dreams laid bare.
Each layer whispers stories vast,
Of journeys taken, shadows cast.

As creation blooms, we watch it grow,
In gentle spirals, evolving flow.
With every breath, we shape our fate,
In the heart of the artist, passion waits.

Unfolding layers, a dance of grace,
In the silence, we find our space.
To build, to break, to softly mend,
In this creation, we find our blend.

So let us peel and layer still,
With every heartbeat, with every will.
In the art of creation, we discover new,
Unfolding paths, each moment true.

Chiaroscuro Collective

In twilight's dance, shadows weave,
A canvas of light, we dare to believe.
Whispers of gray in a world so bright,
Holding the contrast, heart like a kite.

Brush strokes collide in colors so bold,
Stories of lives and tales to be told.
Soft echoes linger in the silent air,
Uniting the fractured, a truth we share.

Every line drawn, a struggle embraced,
In the depths of darkness, our spirits are chased.
From pain to beauty, we rise and fall,
Finding our strength in this chiaroscuro call.

With every shadow, a light shall grow,
Embracing the unknown, we ebb and flow.
Together we stand, in the blend of hues,
Collective creation, our passion imbues.

So let us create, with heart and with soul,
In the dance of existence, we find our whole.
In every dip, every rise, we shall flow,
Chiaroscuro dreams, forever aglow.

The Intersection of Expression

In the heart of the city, voices collide,
A tapestry woven where dreams cannot hide.
Each step is a story, a beat to the rhyme,
Finding our rhythm, transcending the time.

Colors of culture brush vibrant and bold,
Merging our tales, our futures unfold.
Through laughter and sorrow, we paint our arcs,
Every voice a spark igniting the dark.

Expression flows freely, like rivers of thought,
In this intersection, our battles are fought.
With each stroke of passion, our spirits entwined,
Creating a symphony, hearts redefined.

No barriers hold us, together we stand,
Building a bridge with a compassionate hand.
In the pulse of the moment, we find our grace,
The beauty of life, in this shared space.

So let our voices rise, let them soar high,
In this intersection where dreams never die.
With courage and love, our truths we will share,
Together in harmony, embracing the air.

Harmonizing Hurts

In the silence between, where the echoes reside,
We gather our sorrows, no reason to hide.
Every tear tells a tale, every scar sings a song,
In the art of our struggle, we find where we belong.

With fragile notes of hurt, a symphony plays,
We dance with our shadows, through darkened days.
In the warmth of the sorrow, connection we find,
Healing begins when we open our mind.

Each ache is a lesson, a step in the dance,
Learning to lean into love, to take the chance.
Together we rise, in this shared lament,
Transforming our pain, a beautiful blend.

As harmonies linger in the breeze of the night,
We weave a soft blanket, wrap tight in the light.
Through the chords of our heartache, resilience we sound,

In the blend of our voices, true solace is found.

Let the music of healing resound in our chest,
In the arms of our sorrow, we find our rest.
So sing with your heart, let the pains intertwine,
In the harmonizing hurts, together we shine.

The Bouquets of Brushstrokes

In gardens of color, our palettes collide,
Nature's own beauty, with nowhere to hide.
Each brushstroke a petal, each hue a delight,
In the bouquets of moments, pure joy takes flight.

Layered with love, the canvas unfolds,
Whispers of stories, both timid and bold.
A symphony blossoms in the strokes of a hand,
Together we flourish, united we stand.

With petals of laughter, and thorns of despair,
We paint our existence with vibrant care.
Each fragrance of passion, each scent of the night,
In the art of creation, our spirits ignite.

So gather the colors, let's dance in delight,
With every foundation, we reach new height.
In the bouquet of dreams, where the wildflowers play,
We create our own path, in our unique way.

Forever we'll flourish, together as one,
Crafting the beauty, till the day is done.
In the bouquets of brushstrokes, our story remains,
A canvas of hopes, washed in love's veins.

Dreamscapes in Motion

In twilight's hush, dreams begin to dance,
Whispers of time, a fleeting chance.
Stars weave stories, softly they glow,
Binding the night with shimmering flow.

Clouds drift lazily, painted in hue,
A canvas of visions, fresh and new.
Each flicker of light, like a heartbeat's sigh,
Guiding our souls as we softly fly.

Echoes of laughter in shadows, they play,
Chasing the dawn of a brighter day.
With every step in realms unseen,
We chase the dreams where we've never been.

A tapestry woven with threads of gold,
Each moment a treasure, each sight a bold.
Through valleys of wonder, with stars our guide,
In dreamscapes in motion, together we ride.

As morning breaks, the visions may fade,
Yet in our hearts, their magic is laid.
For dreams are the journeys we take in flight,
In the dance of the shadows and beams of light.

Ink and Soul Entwined

With every stroke, the ink takes flight,
Words flow like rivers, day into night.
Pages whisper secrets, stories unfold,
Ink and soul entwined, the truth retold.

In shadows of silence, ideas emerge,
A symphony of thoughts begins to surge.
Hearts bleed on paper, emotions laid bare,
Capturing moments with delicate care.

Each letter a brushstroke, each word a hue,
Creating a portrait, unique and true.
Through passion and pain, the narrative glows,
In ink and in soul, a connection flows.

The ink may dry, but the bond remains,
Lingering echoes of joys and pains.
As stories entwine, like vines they climb,
Ink and soul forever, transcending time.

In the still of the night, the pages call,
Inviting the dreamers to hear it all.
In silence, we ponder, in shadows, we write,
Ink and soul entwined, igniting the night.

Patterns of a Lively Heart

A heart beats boldly, drumming its tune,
In the dance of life, under sun and moon.
Rhythms of joy, in laughter and tears,
Patterns emerge, crafted through years.

With colors alive, the palette expands,
Every emotion, like footprints in sands.
In the tapestry woven of love and despair,
Life's vibrant patterns, exquisite and rare.

Each pulse a reminder, each breath a song,
In the chorus of life, where we all belong.
Through valleys of doubt and mountains of grace,
The heart's patterns flourish, finding their place.

In whispers of kindness, the heart's thread glows,
Binding us gently, wherever it flows.
In the warmth of embrace, the patterns we share,
Unraveling magic, forever laid bare.

So dance to the rhythm, let your heart sway,
In the patterns of life, find your own way.
With each beat, a story, with each turn, a start,
In the beautiful chaos of a lively heart.

Chiaroscuro Serenades

In shadows deep, where secrets sigh,
Light dances softly, a lullaby.
Contrasts of life, in dark and bright,
Chiaroscuro serenades awaken the night.

Between the lines, the silence speaks,
Echoes of longing, truth it seeks.
In the twilight embrace, stories unfold,
Of dreams and desires, both gentle and bold.

Each flicker a whisper, each glow a call,
Painting the silence, revealing it all.
In the balance of space, we find our way,
Through chiaroscuro, dusk turns to day.

Emotions collide, in light and in shade,
Crafting a melody, a serenade.
In the interplay of loss and of gain,
Life's beauty emerges, despite the pain.

So listen, dear heart, to the music within,
In the depths of the shadows, let the light in.
For in every contrast, a truth will ignite,
In chiaroscuro serenades, we find our light.

Tides of Imagination in Bloom

Whispers dance on gentle waves,
Colors swirl in boundless seas.
Thoughts take flight on vibrant breeze,
A canvas stretched where dreams misbehave.

Unfurling petals, soft and bright,
Each hue a story waiting to be known.
Rippling currents shape the light,
As visions craft a world of their own.

Waves of wonder rise and crest,
Unbound by time, they ebb and flow.
In every heart, a hidden quest,
To find the seeds that yearn to grow.

Radiant gardens bloom anew,
Roots entwined with thoughts profound.
In brows of clouds, the dreams break through,
Lost in the silence, beauty is found.

Together, we ride the tides of grace,
In every moment, magic unfolds.
Feelings painted on a timeless space,
As imagination's story, it holds.

The Language of Mixed Dreams

In shadows cast by moonlit glow,
Words collide in secret streams.
Fragments whisper, soft and low,
Weaving tales from silent dreams.

A tapestry of wish and woe,
Woven threads that twist and bend.
Every heartbeat a rhythm slow,
Every glance a chance to mend.

Chasing echoes of fleeting thoughts,
Where fantasies find breathing room.
In tangled realms, our longing rots,
Yet blooms anew in vibrant bloom.

Clouds of doubt, they shift and sway,
Yet clarity drifts on the breeze.
With every dawn, the night gives way,
To the songs of dreams that tease.

We'll paint the skies with every sigh,
Letting colors intermingle and blend.
In the heart of night, we'll fly high,
Speaking the language only we comprehend.

Convergences of Light and Shadow

Morning breaks with gentle grace,
Light and shadow dance entwined.
Realities blend, a fleeting chase,
Secrets linger, undefined.

In the quiet, forms take flight,
Whispers echo through the veil.
As colors meet in soft twilight,
Dreams arise where senses sail.

Silhouettes in twilight's glow,
Harmonies of dusk begin.
Where the wild imaginings flow,
The silent symphonies spin.

Stories etched in shades of grey,
Fragments of the day's soft sigh.
We cherish truths that drift away,
Beneath the painted, endless sky.

At every turn, possibilities,
A dance with fate, a fleeting glance.
In this moment, memories freeze,
As light and shadow take their chance.

The Palette of Modern Musings

Strokes of thought, both bold and bright,
Fill the canvas of the day.
Ideas bloom in morning light,
A vibrant dance where colors play.

Fragments sparked by fleeting dreams,
Shadows cast from visions near.
Every whisper flows with themes,
As the heart learns to draw near.

Palette rich with shades of heart,
Brushes dipped in hopes and fears.
Each creation sets apart,
A story told through laughter, tears.

Mixing echoes of life's refrain,
Harmony in chaos found.
With every stroke, the joy, the pain,
A symphony that knows no bound.

Beneath the layers of the new,
Olds find space to sing and thrive.
In every piece, a part of you,
The palette glows, and dreams arrive.

Embracing the Eclectic

In colors bright, we intertwine,
Threads of culture, each design.
A tapestry of voices loud,
Embracing all, we stand so proud.

From rhythms rich to tastes diverse,
We find the joy, we lift the curse.
In every sound, a story's found,
In unity, our hearts unbound.

The dance of styles, the clash of norms,
In every heartbeat, creativity warms.
Brush strokes wild, a canvas free,
In eclectic beauty, we find glee.

Through laughter shared and struggles faced,
In every difference, love is traced.
Together woven, lives embrace,
In this bright world, we find our place.

So let us sing, let voices rise,
In vibrant hues beneath the skies.
For in the mix, we find our worth,
Embracing eclectic, we birth new earth.

The Chorus of Innovation

In sparks of thought, new visions soar,
Inventive minds that dare explore.
From ancient roots, new branches spread,
A symphony where dreams are fed.

Machines that hum, and ideas ignite,
A chorus sings of future's light.
In every corner, whispers grow,
Together shaping what we know.

The clash of ideas, the merging streams,
In each invention, we weave our dreams.
Through trial and error, paths unfold,
A story of progress waiting to be told.

Collaboration, a dance divine,
Uniting hearts, the stars align.
In every setback, lessons gained,
A chorus of hope that can't be contained.

With hands that build and minds that seek,
Innovation whispers, it dares to speak.
Together roaring, a bold embrace,
The future's song in every space.

Dreamscapes of Disarray

In twilight whispers, shadows play,
Fragments lost in disarray.
Beneath the surface, chaos brews,
In tangled webs, our fears diffuse.

A canvas smeared with thoughts unclear,
Dreams collide, both far and near.
In this wild dance, we often roam,
Finding solace, crafting home.

Yet through the storm, light starts to break,
In muddled paths, we learn to wake.
The beauty found in every flaw,
In dishabille, there's much to draw.

With open hearts, we journey wide,
Navigating waves, we turn the tide.
For in each twist, a lesson lies,
Amidst the mess, our spirit flies.

So let us wander, let us dream,
In tangled truths, life's thread may seam.
Through dreamscapes lost, we find our way,
In vibrant hues of disarray.

Resounding Realism

In everyday tales, our truth resides,
Stories told where the heart abides.
Through trials faced and laughter shared,
In every moment, life declared.

With open eyes, we seek to see,
The world unveiled, a tapestry.
In humble streets and crowded rooms,
Resilience blooms, and hope resumes.

Through simple acts, we bridge the gap,
With kindness woven in every map.
In honest words, connections grow,
In shared realities, we come to know.

Each sunrise brings a brand new chance,
To face the day, to join the dance.
In grit and grace, our paths align,
In resounding truth, our souls entwine.

So lift your voice to life's sweet call,
In every rise, in every fall.
For in this journey, we're not alone,
In every heartbeat, we find our home.

Harmony in Hues

Colors dance in the morning light,
A symphony of shades takes flight.
Whispers of blue, green's embrace,
In nature's palette, we find our place.

Brushstrokes blend in a silent song,
Unity thrives where they all belong.
Each hue tells a story, bold and bright,
Together they form pure delight.

Amidst the chaos, calm resides,
In colors' warmth, our spirit glides.
With every glance, a gentle sigh,
A reminder of beauty, no reason to cry.

When day fades and twilight glows,
The canvas shifts, our hearts it knows.
In dusky tones, dreams intertwine,
A tapestry rich, sublime, divine.

Harmony thrives as shadows blend,
In every moment, colors mend.
Together they weave a tale so grand,
In the heart of the artist's hand.

Transcending Techniques

Lines converge in a graceful sweep,
Crafted with care, their secrets keep.
Where skill meets heart, creation thrives,
In every detail, passion drives.

Tools of artistry, wielded with grace,
Transcend the norm, embrace the space.
Each stroke of genius, a step anew,
Revealing horizons both bright and true.

From canvas vast to sculpted clay,
Innovation blooms, it lights the way.
In every medium, a story flows,
Unfolding beauty, where wonder grows.

Techniques evolve, but soul remains,
Echoes of history in all that pains.
Finding the freedom within the form,
To create a rhythm, to break the norm.

Art speaks boldly, it breaks the mold,
In every creation, a dream unfolds.
With open hearts, we dare to explore,
Transcending techniques, we yearn for more.

Confluence of Creations

In a world where ideas collide,
New visions emerge, like the turning tide.
Craft and concept, hand in hand,
Together they rise, together they stand.

Voices unite, a chorus of mind,
In every creation, a treasure to find.
Different strokes, yet one shared aim,
A tapestry woven in unity's name.

Where boundaries blur and limits fall,
Innovation thrives, answering the call.
In each endeavor, a spark ignites,
Lighting the path to infinite heights.

Collaboration breeds magic anew,
In the gathering forces, visions accrue.
Hearts and hands merged, a radiant stream,
The confluence leads us toward a dream.

From chaos to beauty, we find our way,
A journey of art, where all colors play.
Creating together, we lift each other,
In a world of wonder, we are like no other.

Echoing Each Other

In the silence, voices hum,
Echoes of thoughts, a shared drum.
Resonating truths, profoundly clear,
In the space between, we draw near.

Reflections of self in others' eyes,
Through every moment, we realize.
A dance of souls, in rhythm we flow,
In the warmth of together, our spirits grow.

Words like petals, gently fall,
Each one a whisper, answering the call.
In every story, connections ignite,
Weaving a fabric, so pure, so bright.

Laughter and tears, together we share,
In the echo of life, we find that we care.
Unity formed in the light of the day,
As we walk this journey, come what may.

In the harmony of hearts, we exist,
An endless echo, a beautiful twist.
In every goodbye, in every hello,
Eternal echoes in love's gentle flow.

Palette of Diversity

Each hue a story, bright and bold,
Tales of cultures, dreams unfold.
Unity in every shade,
A vibrant world, together laid.

In rich tones, voices blend,
From every corner, hearts extend.
Cerulean skies and amber fields,
In diversity, life's truth reveals.

Emerald greens and golden sun,
Every color, everyone.
In this palette, we find our place,
Celebrating beauty, love, and grace.

With brush in hand, we craft our fate,
A masterpiece that won't abate.
Threads of heart, stitched with care,
In a canvas broad, we all share.

Together we stand, side by side,
In this mosaic, we won't hide.
Each stroke a testament we leave,
In this palette, we believe.

The Dance of Creation

In whispers soft, the cosmos sways,
Stars ignite in endless plays.
Galaxies spin, twirl with glee,
In the dance of what will be.

Rhythms pulse through time and space,
Each moment holds a sacred grace.
Elements clash and new worlds rise,
In the heartbeat of the skies.

Colors weave in brilliant light,
Darkness gives way to pure delight.
From chaos, order finds its way,
In this dance, night turns to day.

The song of life, a sweet refrain,
In every joy, in every pain.
Creation's breath, a swirling breeze,
In this dance, we'll find our ease.

With every step, a story spins,
In this ballet, life begins.
A cosmic dance that knows no end,
In creation's arms, we transcend.

Colors Collide

When crimson kisses cobalt blue,
A burst of magic, bold and true.
Emeralds blend with twilight's hue,
In the chaos, beauty grew.

Shapes and tones in wild embrace,
Patterns shift, as dreams we chase.
When shadows mix with vibrant light,
A symphony of day and night.

Brushes stroke with fervent zeal,
Artistry begins to heal.
As canvases pulse with vivid claims,
Each collision ignites new flames.

Fragments dance in swirling time,
Life's essence finds its rhyme.
In every clash, a story born,
From dusk to dawn, a world reborn.

Textures merge, horizons bend,
A journey where paths transcend.
Together in this radiant tide,
We find our peace where colors collide.

Tapestry of Imagination

Threads of thought interlace the sky,
Woven dreams that dare to fly.
In fabric rich, ideas twirl,
Crafting visions that unfurl.

With every stitch, a tale unfolds,
Adventures great and whispers bold.
Colors burst in vibrant seams,
A tapestry spun from our dreams.

Patterns dance, rhythm in flow,
An quilt of passion, ebb, and glow.
Weaving hopes into every band,
In this crafty, wondrous land.

Stories join, each thread a voice,
In this tapestry, we rejoice.
For in imagination's art,
We find the fabric of the heart.

Embroidered in love, stitched with care,
A boundless world, everywhere.
In every patch, a spark ignites,
In this tapestry, our spirit lights.

Painting with Sound

Brushstrokes of whispers, colors ablaze,
Notes dancing freely, a symphonic haze.
Echoes of laughter, hues intertwined,
A canvas of memories, vivid and blind.

Harmony flows, like rivers in spring,
Each chord a petal, each rhythm a wing.
Mingling together, we capture the light,
In an opus of moments, an endless delight.

Sounds bloom like flowers, in gardens of air,
Melodies shimmer, in colors so rare.
The brush of the wind, the beat of the night,
A masterpiece born in the heart's pure light.

Echoing chambers of joy and despair,
Every heartbeat a pulse; love's tender care.
Painting with sound, we find our own way,
Creating a world, where night turns to day.

With every crescendo, the story unfolds,
A tale of the heart, in colors so bold.
In the symphony played, we discover our ground,
Life's vivid creation, our painting with sound.

Sculpture of Silence

In stillness, we gather, forming the clay,
Molding the whispers, where shadows play.
Each touch a promise, each pause profound,
A sanctuary built, where calmness is found.

Breath held in moments, like dew on the grass,
Time stretches gently, as echoes pass.
Carving our thoughts in the quiet of night,
A sculpture of silence, where fears take flight.

Figures emerge, from the soft, shapeless mass,
Ghosts of the past, in the silence, they pass.
Stillness resonates, a profound embrace,
In the heart of the void, we find our own space.

Layers of meaning, etched deep in the stone,
The beauty of silence, uniquely our own.
In hushed conversations, connection ignites,
In this tranquil art, we reach higher heights.

Sculpted in quiet, definitions unwind,
The power of stillness, our souls intertwined.
Crafting a world where the chaos is tamed,
In the sculpture of silence, our spirits are named.

Merging Melodies

Two streams of sound, entwined in the air,
A fusion of rhythms, a dance we both share.
Notes glide together, a tapestry spun,
In the heart of the music, we become one.

Fingers on strings, hearts open wide,
We navigate waves, in the ebb and tide.
Voices like water, flow sweetly and free,
Merging our dreams in perfect harmony.

Chords intertwine, like vines on a wall,
Creating a forest where echoes enthrall.
In this vibrant garden, we lose and we find,
A melody woven, where souls are aligned.

Symphonies blossom, like stars in the night,
Guiding our journey, igniting our light.
Together we soar, where the silence gives way,
In merging melodies, we'll forever stay.

A union of hearts, a blend of the sounds,
In the music of love, where connection abounds.
With every note played, another layer unfolds,
In merging melodies, our story is told.

Fragmented Fantasies

Shattered reflections, pieces of dreams,
Caught in the twilight, unraveling seams.
Fragments of moments, scattered and bright,
Painted with echoes of lost, whispered light.

Each shard a memory, a tale to be told,
In the tapestry woven, both fragile and bold.
Dreams breaking open, like waves on the shore,
In the chaos of feelings, we yearn for much more.

Clouds merge with whispers, a sky full of sighs,
In the depth of the night, truth softly applies.
Illusions are dancing, like shadows on sand,
Fragmented fantasies, together we stand.

Time spills like water, through fingers it flows,
In the ruins of silence, our spirit still glows.
Embracing the chaos, we build from the fall,
In fragmented fantasies, we rise through it all.

We weave through the pieces, embracing the pain,
Finding in darkness, the strength to sustain.
Together we thrive, through the dreams that we've spun,
In fragmented fantasies, our journey's begun.